BY ALLAN MOREY

THE CLEVELAND
BROWNS
STORY

BELLWETHER MEDIA · MINNEAPOLIS, MN

TM

Are you ready to take it to the extreme? Torque books thrust you into the action-packed world of sports, vehicles, mystery, and adventure. These books may include dirt, smoke, fire, and chilling tales. **WARNING**: read at your own risk.

This edition first published in 2017 by Bellwether Media, Inc.

No part of this publication may be reproduced in whole or in part without written permission of the publisher. For information regarding permission, write to Bellwether Media, Inc., Attention: Permissions Department, 5357 Penn Avenue South, Minneapolis, MN 55419.

Library of Congress Cataloging-in-Publication Data

Names: Morey, Allan, author.
Title: The Cleveland Browns Story / by Allan Morey.
Description: Minneapolis, MN : Bellwether Media, Inc., 2017. | Series:
   Torque: NFL Teams | Includes index.
Identifiers: LCCN 2015045393 | ISBN 9781626173620 (hardcover : alk. paper)
Subjects: LCSH: Cleveland Browns (Football team)–History–Juvenile literature.
Classification: LCC GV956.C6 M66 2017 | DDC 796.332/640977132–dc23
LC record available at http://lccn.loc.gov/2015045393

Printed in the United States of America, North Mankato, MN.

TABLE OF CONTENTS

BEATING A RIVAL 4

AN EARLY PRO FOOTBALL DYNASTY 8

THEN TO NOW 14

BROWNS TIMELINE 18

TEAM SUPERSTARS 20

FANS AND TEAM CULTURE 24

MORE ABOUT THE BROWNS 28

GLOSSARY 30

TO LEARN MORE 31

INDEX 32

It is September 16, 2007. The Cleveland Browns face the Cincinnati Bengals. The teams are big **rivals**. Both are from Ohio.

Jamal Lewis

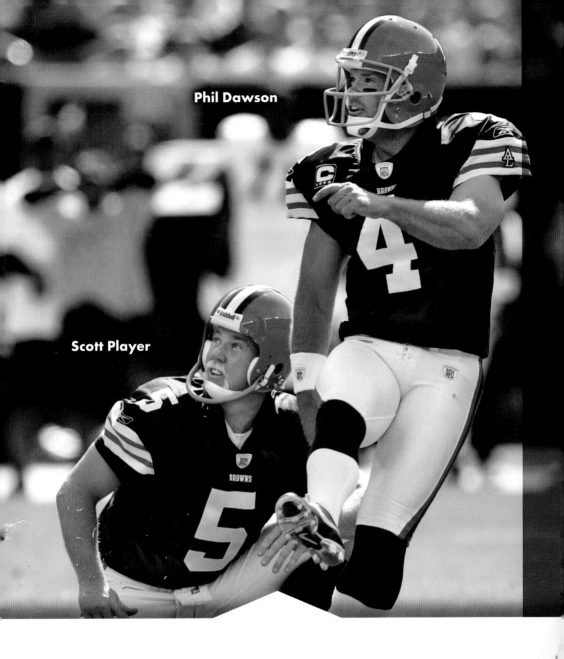

Phil Dawson

Scott Player

The Bengals get the first score of the game. Their **quarterback** tosses a 13-yard touchdown pass. Then the Browns kick two field goals before the end of the first quarter.

Derek
Anderson

In the second quarter, the score explodes! Quarterback Derek Anderson throws three touchdowns for the Browns. The Bengals score two more touchdowns. At the half, the Browns lead 27 to 21.

But the scoring does not stop. When the game ends, it is 51 to 45. Browns win!

SCORING TERMS

END ZONE

the area at each end of a football field; a team scores by entering the opponent's end zone with the football.

EXTRA POINT

a score that occurs when a kicker kicks the ball between the opponent's goal posts after a touchdown is scored; 1 point.

FIELD GOAL

a score that occurs when a kicker kicks the ball between the opponent's goal posts; 3 points.

SAFETY

a score that occurs when a player on offense is tackled behind his own goal line; 2 points for defense.

TOUCHDOWN

a score that occurs when a team crosses into its opponent's end zone with the football; 6 points.

TWO-POINT CONVERSION

a score that occurs when a team crosses into its opponent's end zone with the football after scoring a touchdown; 2 points.

The Browns had a strong start as a team. They were an early **dynasty**. In the 1940s, they ruled the All-America Football Conference (AAFC). They won four titles.

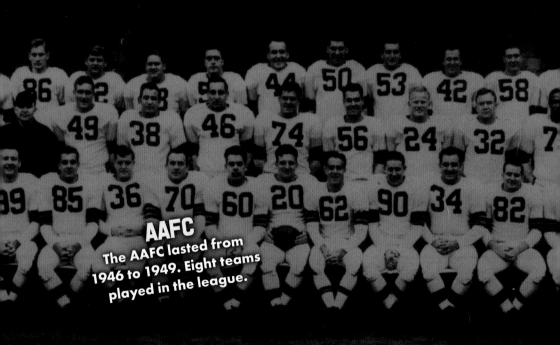

CLEVELAND BROWNS FOOTBALL C

AAFC CHAMPIONS 1946-47-48-49

AAFC

The AAFC lasted from 1946 to 1949. Eight teams played in the league.

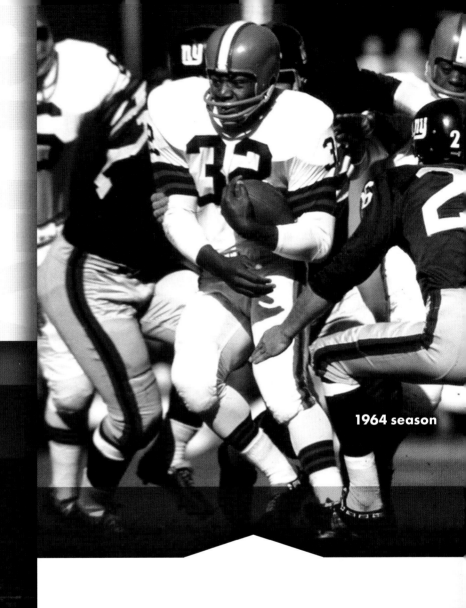
1964 season

Then the Browns started playing in the National Football League (NFL). And they kept winning. They won three NFL titles in the 1950s and a fourth in 1964!

Cleveland sits on Lake Erie's southern shore. Close to the water is the Browns' home, FirstEnergy Stadium. Before it opened, the Browns shared the old Lakefront Stadium with Cleveland's baseball team, the Indians.

The most famous area in FirstEnergy Stadium is at the east end zone. The rowdiest fans sit in the Dawg Pound located there.

FIRSTENERGY STADIUM

CLEVELAND, OHIO

N
W + E
S

THIS IS OUR HOUSE

PLAYOFFS ARE IN SIGHT!

11

The Browns joined the NFL in 1950. They play in the American Football **Conference** (AFC). They are in the North **Division**. The Pittsburgh Steelers, Baltimore Ravens, and Cincinnati Bengals also belong to the division.

The Browns and Steelers are the biggest AFC North rivals. They have played each other more than 120 times!

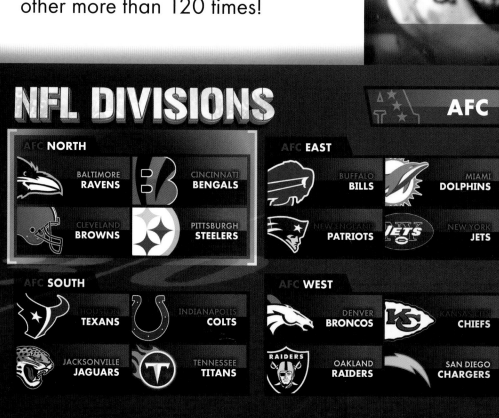

NFL DIVISIONS

AFC

AFC NORTH

BALTIMORE **RAVENS**

CINCINNATI **BENGALS**

CLEVELAND **BROWNS**

PITTSBURGH **STEELERS**

AFC EAST

BUFFALO **BILLS**

MIAMI **DOLPHINS**

NEW ENGLAND **PATRIOTS**

NEW YORK **JETS**

AFC SOUTH

HOUSTON **TEXANS**

INDIANAPOLIS **COLTS**

JACKSONVILLE **JAGUARS**

TENNESSEE **TITANS**

AFC WEST

DENVER **BRONCOS**

KANSAS CITY **CHIEFS**

OAKLAND **RAIDERS**

SAN DIEGO **CHARGERS**

NFC

NFC NORTH

 CHICAGO **BEARS**

 DETROIT **LIONS**

 GREEN BAY **PACKERS**

 MINNESOTA **VIKINGS**

NFC EAST

DALLAS **COWBOYS**

 NEW YORK **GIANTS**

 PHILADELPHIA **EAGLES**

 WASHINGTON **REDSKINS**

NFC SOUTH

 ATLANTA **FALCONS**

 CAROLINA **PANTHERS**

 NEW ORLEANS **SAINTS**

 TAMPA BAY **BUCCANEERS**

NFC WEST

 ARIZONA **CARDINALS**

LOS ANGELES **RAMS**

 SAN FRANCISCO **49ERS**

 SEATTLE **SEAHAWKS**

The Browns started out with head coach Paul Brown. He led the team to all four AAFC titles. No other team ever claimed an AAFC Championship.

BROWN FOR BROWN
Cleveland's team was named the Browns after Coach Brown.

14

NFL CHAMPIONSHIP
DECEMBER 24, 1950

People did not think the team would do as well in the NFL. But Coach Brown proved them wrong. The Browns won the NFL Championship their very first year in the league!

A big change came in 1996.
Browns owner Art Modell moved
the team. He took the players
to Baltimore, Maryland. But
the NFL did not let Modell take
the team name. So the Browns
became the Ravens.

In 1999, NFL football returned to Cleveland. The city was given an **expansion team**. The Browns were back!

2008 season

BROWNS
TIMELINE

1946
Joined the AAFC

1950
Joined the NFL

1954
Won the NFL Championship, beating the Detroit Lions

56 FINAL SCORE **10**

1956
Drafted Hall-of-Fame fullback Jim Brown

1950
Won their first NFL Championship, beating the Los Angeles Rams

30 FINAL SCORE **28**

1955
Won the NFL Championship, beating the Los Angeles Rams

38 FINAL SCORE **14**

1964

Won the NFL Championship, beating the Baltimore Colts

27 FINAL SCORE **0**

2007

Drafted offensive lineman Joe Thomas

1996

Relocated to Baltimore and became the Ravens

1985

Drafted star quarterback Bernie Kosar

1999

Returned to Cleveland as an NFL expansion team

BROWNS

Over the years, fans have cheered for some talented Browns. **Fullback** Jim Brown **rushed** for 12,312 yards from 1957 to 1965. Then Leroy Kelly became the strong ball carrier.

Leroy
Kelly

Jim
Brown

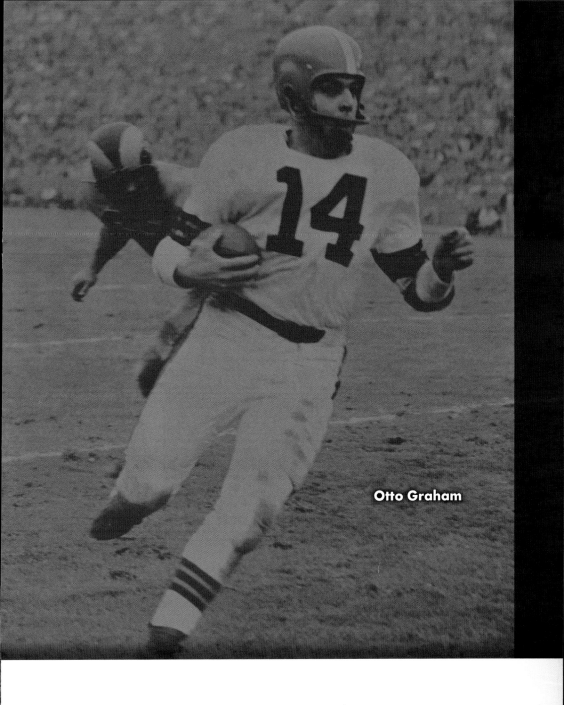

Otto Graham

Quarterback Otto Graham played in the 1940s and 1950s. He led the team to seven championships.

In the 1980s and 1990s, quarterback Bernie Kosar brought the team's passing attack. He threw for 489 yards in a **playoff** game in 1987. This is a playoff record!

Hall-of-Fame **tight end** Ozzie Newsome caught many of Kosar's passes. During his NFL career, he caught 662 passes!

TEAM GREATS

OTTO GRAHAM
QUARTERBACK
1946-1955

JIM BROWN
FULLBACK
1957-1965

LEROY KELLY
RUNNING BACK
1964-1973

Joe Haden

JOE AND JOE

Today, the Browns have Joe Thomas and Joe Haden. Thomas is a strong offensive tackle. Haden shuts down almost any wide receiver.

OZZIE NEWSOME
TIGHT END
1978-1990

BERNIE KOSAR
QUARTERBACK
1985-1993

JOE THOMAS
OFFENSIVE TACKLE
2007-PRESENT

In 1985, **cornerback** Hanford Dixon nicknamed the Browns' **defense**. He called them the "Dawgs." He had his teammates bark after big plays.

Hanford Dixon

BROWNIES
Fans bark during the team chant. They shout, "Here we go, Brownies. Here we go! Woof! Woof!"

This caught on with the fans. They would also bark. Some fans started wearing dog masks. The area where these fans sat became known as the Dawg Pound.

Fans have had little to cheer about in recent years. First, the team moved to Baltimore. Now back, the Browns have struggled to make the playoffs.

Yet fans stay loyal to their Browns. They remember the team's past greatness. They believe the Browns will be the best in the NFL again!

MORE ABOUT THE
BROWNS

Team name:
Cleveland Browns

Team name explained:
Named after Paul Brown,
the team's first head coach
and general manager

Nicknames:
Kardiac Kids, Dawgs

Joined NFL: 1950
(AAFC from 1946-1949)

Conference: AFC

Division: North

**Main rivals: Pittsburgh Steelers,
Cincinnati Bengals**

100% DAWG POUND

Hometown:
Cleveland, Ohio

Training camp location:
Cleveland Browns Training Facility, Berea, Ohio

CLEVELAND

OHIO

N
W + E
S

Home stadium name:
FirstEnergy Stadium

Stadium opened: 1999

Seats in stadium: 67,431

Logo: The Cleveland Browns helmet

Colors: Orange, brown, white

Chomps

Name for fan base: Dawg Pound

Mascots: Chomps and Swagger

Swagger

GLOSSARY

conference—a large grouping of sports teams that often play one another

cornerback—a player on defense whose main job is to stop wide receivers from catching passes; a cornerback is positioned outside of the linebackers.

defense—the group of players who try to stop the opposing team from scoring

division—a small grouping of sports teams that often play one another; usually there are several divisions of teams in a conference.

dynasty—a team that succeeds for many years

expansion team—a new team added to a sports league

fullback—a player on offense whose main jobs are to block and to take handoffs from the quarterback

playoff—a game played after the regular NFL season is over; playoff games determine which teams play in the Super Bowl.

quarterback—a player on offense whose main job is to throw and hand off the ball

rivals—teams that are long-standing opponents

rushed—ran with the ball

tight end—a player on offense whose main jobs are to catch the ball and block for teammates

TO LEARN MORE

AT THE LIBRARY

Burgess, Zack. *Meet the Cleveland Browns*. Chicago, Ill.: Norwood House Press, 2016.

Wilner, Barry. *Football's Top 10 Running Backs*. Berkeley Heights, N.J.: Enslow Publishers, 2011.

Wyner, Zach. *Cleveland Browns*. New York, N.Y.: AV2 by Weigl, 2015.

ON THE WEB

Learning more about the Cleveland Browns is as easy as 1, 2, 3.

1. Go to www.factsurfer.com.

2. Enter "Cleveland Browns" into the search box.

3. Click the "Surf" button and you will see a list of related web sites.

With factsurfer.com, finding more information is just a click away.

INDEX

All-America Football Conference
   (AAFC), 8, 14, 28

Baltimore, Maryland, 16, 26

Brown, Paul (head coach), 14,
   15, 28

championship, 8, 9, 14, 15, 21

Cleveland, Ohio, 10, 11, 17, 29

colors, 29

conference, 12, 13, 28

Dawg Pound, 10, 25, 29

division, 12, 13, 28

fans, 10, 20, 25, 26, 27, 29

FirstEnergy Stadium, 10, 29

Lakefront Stadium, 10

logo, 29

mascots, 29

Modell, Art (owner), 16

name, 14, 16, 28

nicknames, 24, 26, 28

players, 4, 5, 6, 16, 20, 21, 22,
   23, 24

playoff, 22, 26

positions, 5, 6, 20, 21, 22, 23, 24

Pro Football Hall of Fame, 22

record, 22

rivals, 4, 5, 6, 12, 28

scoring terms, 5, 6, 7, 10

timeline, 18-19

traditions, 24, 25

training camp, 29

vs. Cincinnati Bengals
   (September 16, 2007), 4-7